The Guggenheim Museum Bilbao

MUSEUMS OF THE WORLD

By Lauren Diemer and
Heather Kissock

www.av2books.com

AV[2] provides enriched content that supplements and complements this book. Weigl's AV[2] books strive to create inspired learning and engage young minds in a total learning experience.

Your AV[2] Media Enhanced books come alive with...

Audio
Listen to sections of the book read aloud.

Key Words
Study vocabulary, and complete a matching word activity.

Video
Watch informative video clips.

Quizzes
Test your knowledge.

Embedded Weblinks
Gain additional information for research.

Slide Show
View images and captions, and prepare a presentation.

Try This!
Complete activities and hands-on experiments.

... and much, much more!

Go to **www.av2books.com**, and enter this book's unique code.

BOOK CODE

Y673856

AV[2] by Weigl brings you media enhanced books that support active learning.

Published by AV[2] by Weigl
350 5th Avenue, 59th Floor
New York, NY 10118

Websites: www.av2books.com   www.weigl.com

Library of Congress Cataloging-in-Publication Data
Diemer, Lauren.
  The Guggenheim Museum Bilbao/ Lauren Diemer and Heather Kissock.
     pages cm. -- (Museums of the world)
ISBN 978-1-4896-3240-1 (hardcover : alk. paper) -- ISBN 978-1-4896-3241-8 (softcover : alk. paper) --
ISBN 978-1-4896-3242-5 (single-user ebk.) -- ISBN 978-1-4896-3243-2 (multi-user ebk.)
1. Museo Guggenheim Bilbao--Juvenile literature. 2. Art museums--Spain--Bilbao--Juvenile literature.
3. Bilbao (Spain)--Buildings, structures, etc.--Juvenile literature. I. Title.
 N3412.4.D54 2014
  709.04'00744663--dc23
                  2014038745

Printed in Brainerd, Minnesota, in the United States of America
1 2 3 4 5 6 7 8 9 0 18 17 16 15 14

122014
WEP051214

Editor: Heather Kissock
Designer: Dean Pickup

Every reasonable effort has been made to trace ownership and to obtain permission to reprint copyright material. The publishers would be pleased to have any errors or omissions brought to their attention so that they may be corrected in subsequent printings.

Weigl acknowledges Getty Images, Alamy, Corbis, Newscom, Dreamstime, and iStock as its primary image suppliers for this title.

Contents

What Is the Guggenheim Museum Bilbao?

With its glittering panels and sweeping curves, the Guggenheim Museum in Bilbao, Spain, is one of the most stunning museums in the world. Created specifically to house modern art, the Guggenheim Bilbao is often considered a work of art itself. Its bold exterior hints at the exciting artwork found within its walls. The Guggenheim Bilbao's **collection** is eclectic. Its works range from traditional paintings to large video **installations**. It is a museum designed to make visitors reconsider their definition of art.

The Guggenheim Bilbao is part of a network of museums founded by the Solomon R. Guggenheim Foundation. Other Guggenheim museums are located in New York City and Venice, Italy. A fourth museum is scheduled to open in Abu Dhabi, in the United Arab Emirates, in 2017. All of the Guggenheim museums are committed to engaging people in discussions about art, **architecture**, and other forms of visual culture so that they can gain a deeper understanding of the visual arts. Each of the museums pays special attention to modern and contemporary art.

The Guggenheim Bilbao sits alongside the Nervión River, where its titantium and glass exterior reflects the movement of the water.

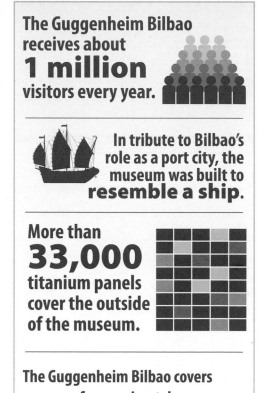

The Guggenheim Bilbao receives about **1 million** visitors every year.

In tribute to Bilbao's role as a port city, the museum was built to **resemble a ship.**

More than **33,000** titanium panels cover the outside of the museum.

The Guggenheim Bilbao covers an area of approximately **258,334 square feet** (24,000 square meters).

History of the Guggenheim Bilbao

The Guggenheim Bilbao was built as part of a city-wide redevelopment plan. Bilbao had long been an important manufacturing and shipping hub. Local leaders felt that developing the cultural side of the city would encourage more investment. Building a world-class museum in the city was a key part of this plan. To ensure that the museum would have international stature, the planners sought the expertise of the Guggenheim Foundation, inviting the foundation's director to visit Bilbao in 1991. By the end of his visit, an agreement to build the museum had been signed.

New York's Solomon R. Guggenheim Museum was the first to be built by the foundation. It was completed in 1959.

1991 The Solomon R. Guggenheim Foundation signs an agreement to build a museum in Bilbao.

1992 A committee is established to oversee the museum's construction.

1990　　**1991**　　**1992**　　**1993**

1991 A design competition is held. Frank O. Gehry is selected as the museum's architect in July.

1993 The **groundbreaking** ceremony is held on October 22.

Bilbao is the capital city of the Spanish province called Bizkaia. The city has a population of more than one million people.

1997 After two weeks of **inaugural** activities, the Guggenheim Bilbao opens to the public on October 19.

2000 The Guggenheim Bilbao is named European Museum of the Year.

2010 The museum opens its new orientation center called Zero Espazioa. The room features interactive tools that allow visitors to design their own museum tour.

1995   2000   2005   2010

2001 The museum's storage area is remodeled to provide more space for its growing collection.

1999 The museum launches its website.

2009 The Guggenheim Bilbao releases its first publication about the works in its collection.

Key People

The Guggenheim Bilbao came to be as a result of several forward thinkers. These people believed in the power of art and the need to expand its reach to new settings and new audiences. Their dedication to these beliefs resulted in a museum that is known throughout the world for its fresh approach to the visual arts.

Solomon R. Guggenheim (1861–1949)

Even though Solomon R. Guggenheim was not alive to see the Guggenheim Bilbao built, his influence over the project is obvious. The museum is named after him and was funded by his organization. Guggenheim was born in Philadelphia, Pennsylvania. He received his early schooling there before going to Europe to study business. When he returned to the United States, he began working for his family's mining business. His success in mining allowed him to develop a large art collection. Wanting to share his love of art with others, he established the Solomon R. Guggenheim Foundation in 1937. Its goal was to promote and encourage art and art education. The foundation honors that mandate to this day.

To share his collection with the public, Solomon R. Guggenheim originally put it on display in his apartment at New York's Plaza Hotel.

Thomas Krens (1946–Present)

As director of the Solomon R. Guggenheim Foundation, Thomas Krens played an instrumental role in getting the museum built. He not only arranged the agreement to build the Guggenheim Bilbao, but also selected the project's architect. Krens had worked as an arts educator in New York and Massachusetts before being hired by the Guggenheim Foundation in 1988. As director, Krens worked to raise the organization's profile internationally. He did this by developing **satellite museums**, such as the Guggenheim Bilbao.

Thomas Krens left his position as director of the Guggenheim Foundation in 2008 to oversee the development of the new Guggenheim museum in Abu Dhabi.

Frank O. Gehry (1929–Present)

Frank O. Gehry showed an early interest in architecture. When he was growing up in Ontario, Canada, Gehry would construct model buildings using items from his grandfather's hardware store. In 1947, Gehry moved to Los Angeles to study architecture at the University of Southern California. One of his first construction projects was the remodeling of his own home. The innovative techniques he used attracted much attention, and he was soon designing buildings for large companies and organizations. Besides the Guggenheim Bilbao, Gehry is also responsible for designing the Walt Disney Concert Hall in Los Angeles and the Dancing House in Prague.

Frank O. Gehry is known for his use of unconventional materials in his buildings, a throwback to his childhood days.

Juan Ignacio Vidarte (1956–present)

Juan Ignacio Vidarte was hired to oversee the construction of the Guggenheim Bilbao. He later became the museum's director general. Born in Bilbao, Vidarte graduated from the city's University of Deusto with a degree in economics and business studies. He then continued his studies at the Massachusetts Institute of Technology in the United States. Upon returning to Spain, he began working as the director of the Institute for Regional Research in Bizkaia. This led to director positions with other similar organizations. Vidarte has played a key role in making the Guggenheim Bilbao one of the world's best-known museums.

In 2008, Juan Ignacio Vidarte became the deputy director for Global Strategies at the Guggenheim Foundation. In this role, he seeks out new projects for the foundation.

The Guggenheim Bilbao Today

The Guggenheim Bilbao has earned a solid reputation among both the general public and the museum community for its ability to engage people in discussions about art. Its efforts toward this goal have brought the museum many accolades. It has also won several awards for its value as both a tourist attraction and an international art institution. The Guggenheim Bilbao continues to seek new art forms to **exhibit** and new ways to attract visitors. In recent years, it has developed new educational programs, hosted an Asian art **symposium**, and received recognition for its environmental policies. All the while, it has continued to add new works to its collection so that it can continue to showcase the scope and depth of modern art in the world.

People enter the galleries of the Guggenheim Bilbao through the atrium. This area covers 3,229 square feet (300 sq. m) and has a height of 164 feet (50 meters).

Second and Third Floors

Permanent and temporary exhibits are distributed throughout the museum's gallery spaces on the second and third floors. They are rotated and repurposed as needed.

Plaza

Visitors can view art before they even enter the museum. The plaza area in front of the museum features several large-scale sculptures.

First Floor

The largest gallery spaces are found on the first floor. It is here that most of the museum's large-scale artworks are exhibited.

Atrium

The atrium forms the center of the museum and connects to all of the galleries.

Touring the Guggenheim Bilbao

The Guggenheim Bilbao has approximately 118,400 square feet (11,000 sq. m) of exhibition space. This space is separated into 20 galleries on three floors. Each gallery's shape indicates the era of the art found within it. Rectangular galleries display works from the early stages of the modernist **movement**. **Asymmetrical** galleries feature more recent art forms.

The Riverfront Terrace

A walk along the museum's riverfront terrace gives visitors an opportunity to see how the Guggenheim Bilbao was built to fit into the urban landscape, as well as enhance it. The terrace features several unique works of art that were designed specifically to be exhibited outdoors.

The terrace surrounds an artificial pond. This pond is also an exhibit area, featuring artworks that require a watery environment.

Gallery 104 is sometimes referred to as the Fish Gallery because of its shape.

Gallery 104 Typically entered from the first floor, Gallery 104 takes up an entire wing of the building. The gallery was originally used to display temporary exhibits, but is now home to a sculpture called *The Matter of Time*. The sculpture is so large that viewers are encouraged to take an elevator to the second floor to better understand the scope of the work.

Film and Video Gallery Located on the first floor, this gallery is a permanent space devoted to film and video installations. The exhibits themselves change throughout the year. However, there is usually only one installation on exhibit at any given time.

In 2014, the Guggenheim Bilbao hosted a video installation by Japanese-American artist Yoko Ono.

The Tower When designing the museum, Frank O. Gehry wanted to link it to its surroundings. To do this, he added a tower to the end of Gallery 104. The gallery runs underneath the city's La Salve Bridge, and the tower rises above it on the other side. In this way, the museum is linked to the city.

The Guggenheim Bilbao's tower contains a staircase that takes visitors to and from the La Salve Bridge.

The atrium is topped with a skylight in the shape of a **metal flower**.

Each part of the Guggenheim is **connected to** and **divided from** the next using glass curtain walls.

Construction of the museum cost **$89 million**.

Gallery 104 is the world's **LARGEST** gallery space. It measures **426 feet** (130 m) long and **98 feet** (30 m) wide.

The titanium panels that cover the museum have been guaranteed to last for **100 years**.

The entrance to the museum sits **52 feet** (16 m) **below** the city of Bilbao.

Puppy is often called a giant chia pet because of its growing blooms.

Snake, a sculpture by Richard Serra, weighs about **180 tons** (163 tonnes).

180 TONS

Jenny Holzer's *Installation for Bilbao* features

9 LED signboards

that are each more than **40 feet** (12 m) tall.

A sculpture called *F.O.G.* uses **1,000** **water nozzles** to send a misty cloud across the plaza.

Humans, a work by Christian Boltanski, is made up of more than **1,200** photographs.

The Matter of Time is made up of **7** individual sculptures measuring up to **14 feet** (4 m) in height.

Treasures of the Guggenheim Bilbao

The Guggenheim Bilbao exhibits works by artists from all over the world. These works showcase the various movements within modern art, ranging from the **abstract expressionism** of post-war America to the cutting-edge works that are being created today. The museum also devotes much of its exhibit space to works by **Basque** artists. The city of Bilbao is located in the heart of Spain's Basque region.

By viewing the works on display in the Guggenheim Bilbao, visitors can see how modern art has evolved over the years, from paintings and sculptures to the digital installations of today.

Maman One of the Guggenheim's best-known works is *Maman* by France's Louise Bourgeois. *Maman* was created as a tribute to the artist's mother, who was a weaver. The 30-foot (9-m) tall sculpture shows a spider, a creature known for weaving webs. It is made from stainless steel, bronze, and marble.

Maman *is located outside of the museum, on the walkway near the riverfront terrace.*

One Hundred and Fifty Multicolored Marilyns

Created by renowned American **pop artist** Andy Warhol, this work features images of 1950s movie icon Marilyn Monroe. The work was created to draw attention to the public's fascination with celebrity. It measures 34 feet 6 inches (10.5 m) in length.

Warhol used a technique called silkscreening to create One Hundred and Fifty Multicolored Marilyns.

Puppy Located on the plaza outside of the museum, *Puppy* was created by American artist Jeff Koons. The 43-foot (13 m) tall steel sculpture shows a West Highland White Terrier covered with bedding plants. Its flowery appearance is a reference to the gardens that surrounded the great houses of 18th-century Europe.

Puppy *is often said to be standing guard over the museum because he stands beside its entrance.*

Villa Borghese Dutch artist Willem de Kooning painted *Villa Borghese* to reflect the mood of the Italian landscape. The title refers to a park in Rome. The bold, sweeping strokes of the paint showcase the abstract expressionist style of the 1950s and 1960s.

De Kooning spent five months living in Rome. He painted Villa Borghese upon returning to his home in the United States.

Collection Conservation

The Guggenheim Bilbao houses some of the world's most important modern artworks. Museum staff want to ensure that the pieces in the museum's collection remain in good condition. This will allow future generations to view the works and understand how they fit into the evolution of art. Professionals called conservators are responsible for the repairs and upkeep of the art. The Guggenheim Bilbao has an entire department of conservators who are trained to understand the unique conditions needed to keep each piece safe.

Light People need light to view works of art. However, light can cause significant damage to artworks, especially paintings. Colors can fade, and paint can become dry and start to chip. Conservators must determine the effect that light has on the materials used to create the work. They may use timers to control the amount of light. They may also put the work into storage for a while to give it a rest from the light.

Several of the Guggenheim Bilbao's galleries use natural light, as well as artificial light, to showcase the works inside.

Controlling Humidity Conservators must monitor **humidity** levels in the museum to ensure that its works are not exposed to too much moisture. High humidity levels can cause mold to form on some materials. This can result in irreversible damage to works of art. When the Guggenheim Bilbao was built, special attention was paid to air flow. Each gallery has its own air handling room. This helps control humidity levels throughout the museum.

Humidity is a major concern at the Guggenheim Bilbao. The city's climate is naturally humid, and the building stands next to a river. This increases the amount of moisture in the air.

Conservators play a key role in determining how and where a work of art will be installed. They often supervise and participate in the installation itself.

Cleaning Artwork placed in public viewing areas will become dirty over time. Dust, grime, and pollution can all have a negative effect on a work of art. Conservators constantly review the works on display to determine if a piece needs to be cleaned. Dust is removed using brushes, cotton swabs, and low-suction vacuums. For a deeper cleaning, conservators sometimes apply special **solvents** or **aqueous** solutions to the works.

Cotton swabs are often used to apply solvents and aqueous solutions to delicate surfaces.

Pest Control Insects, mice, and microscopic organisms can enter a museum in a variety of ways. If they come into contact with works of art, they can eat through the materials and cause permanent damage. The Guggenheim Bilbao has several works that are made from **organic** materials, which can attract insects. When insects are found, the artwork involved is quickly isolated. Insecticides are then used to rid the exhibit area and the work itself of the pests.

Artworks made from organic materials, such as Puppy, have special maintenance needs.

The Guggenheim Bilbao in the World

The Guggenheim Bilbao works hard to maintain its international presence. It reaches out to people and organizations, both locally and in other countries, to educate and enlighten them about modern art. Museum staff are continually working to develop new programs and initiatives that help people access information about the museum's collection.

Education Programs The Guggenheim Bilbao has developed several programs for people visiting the museum. Tour guides are available to take small groups through exhibits. Art classes and workshops are held throughout the year. There are also programs that take place outside the museum. The *Learning Through Art* program sends artists into schools, where they help teachers develop art projects for their classes. The museum runs a similar program for children in local hospitals.

The Guggenheim Bilbao's interpretive guides provide insight into works that may not be easily understood at first glance.

Traveling Exhibits Throughout the year, the Guggenheim Bilbao brings in exhibits that originated with other museums. As part of the Guggenheim museum system, the Bilbao shows many exhibits from the New York and Venice museums. However, the museum has also formed relationships with other museums that share its goals to educate people about modern art. In showing these exhibits or individual works at the Guggenheim Bilbao, the museum is allowing them to reach a wider audience.

The Guggenheim Bilbao also sends pieces from its collection to other museums. In 2005, some of its works were displayed in a museum in Rome, Italy.

Online Community

People from all over the world can access the Guggenheim Bilbao on the internet. The museum's website provides information about the collection, current exhibitions, programs, and activities. An online app provides people with interactive maps, audio and video guides, and digital images of works in the collection. The museum is also active on Facebook, Twitter, and YouTube.

The Guggenheim Bilbao's website offers people the opportunity to plan their visit to the museum. The site includes several tour plan options.

Publications

The museum reaches out to its audience through a variety of publications. Visitors to the Guggenheim Bilbao have access to the museum's magazine, which provides information about current exhibits and activities. People can also sign up to receive a monthly newsletter, which keeps readers up to date on events taking place at the museum. In recent years, the museum has started a book publishing program. Topics have ranged from works in the collection to the story behind the museum's construction.

Most of the Guggenheim Bilbao's publications can be found in the gift shop, which is located on all three floors of the museum.

Looking to the Future

The Guggenheim Bilbao continues to seek new ways to promote art and encourage people to interact with it. Following the example set by the Solomon R. Guggenheim Foundation, the Guggenheim Bilbao has plans to create a satellite museum of its own on the edges of a nature reserve in Urdaibai, Spain. While the museum will show exhibits from the Bilbao collection, it will also be a place for artists to explore the connection between art, nature, and landscapes.

The Urdaibai Biosphere Reserve is best known for its marshland. It covers approximately 85 square miles (220 square kilometers) and includes the fishing town of Bermeo.

The museum is also taking an interest in developing future arts leaders. It has recently formed a partnership with the University of the Basque Country to participate in a graduate studies program that focuses on contemporary art conservation and exhibition. In cooperation with the University of Deusto and New York University, the museum has also launched the International Leadership Program in Visual Arts Management. This program will provide arts leaders with the tools and knowledge they need to manage an international visual arts organization in the 21st century.

The University of Deusto is located in Bilbao. It was founded in 1886 to serve members of the Basque community.

Activity

The curator plays a very important role in a museum. He or she decides what pieces will be exhibited in a museum and where artworks will be displayed. Imagine you are the curator of the Guggenheim Bilbao. There are two different styles of galleries in the museum. These are traditional rectangular galleries and asymmetrical galleries.

Take a look at the images below of various works in the Guggenheim Bilbao's collection. In which style of gallery would you place each of these works? Provide a brief explanation about why you feel that certain artworks should be shown in one style of gallery instead of the other. There is no right or wrong answer. Your decisions should be based on the ideas you want to present in your exhibit and how you want people to react to the art.

Guggenheim Bilbao Quiz

1 In what country is the Guggenheim Bilbao located?

2 Who designed the building that houses the museum?

3 Which part of the museum is linked to all of the galleries?

4 Which sculpture guards the entrance to the museum?

5 How much did the construction of the museum cost?

ANSWERS:

1. Spain **2.** Frank O. Gehry **3.** The atrium **4.** *Puppy* **5.** $89 million

Key Words

abstract expressionism: an art form that expresses emotion

aqucous: of, likc, or containing water

architecture: the design of buildings and other structures

asymmetrical: having parts that are unequal in some respect

Basque: a person living in northern Spain

collection: works of art or other items collected for exhibit and study in a museum, and kept as part of its holdings

exhibit: to put on public display

groundbreaking: the breaking of soil at the start of a construction project

humidity: moisture in the air

inaugural: marking the beginning of something

installations: works of art made up of multiple components that are exhibited in a large space

movement: a tendency or trend

organic: of or relating to living matter

pop artist: someone who creates art that is based on popular culture and mass media

satellite museums: museums that are physically separated from but dependent on another museum

solvents: substances in which other substances are dissolved

symposium: a conference or meeting to discuss a specific subject

Index

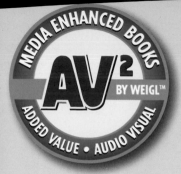

Log on to www.av2books.com

AV² by Weigl brings you media enhanced books that support active learning. Go to www.av2books.com, and enter the special code found on page 2 of this book. You will gain access to enriched and enhanced content that supplements and complements this book. Content includes video, audio, weblinks, quizzes, a slide show, and activities.

AV² Online Navigation

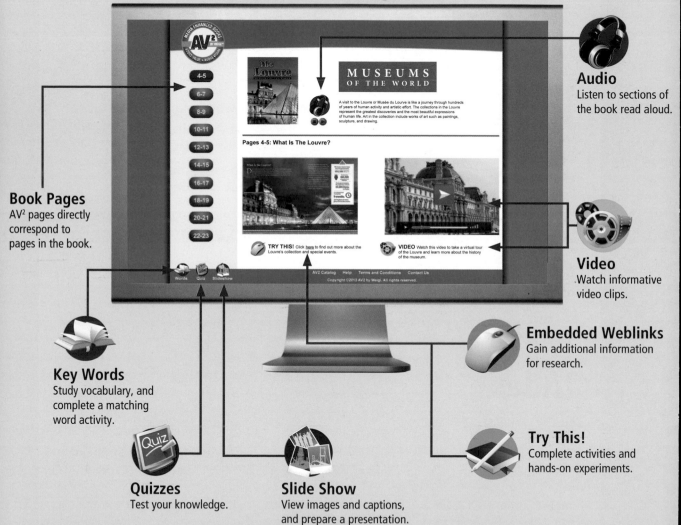

Audio
Listen to sections of the book read aloud.

Video
Watch informative video clips.

Embedded Weblinks
Gain additional information for research.

Try This!
Complete activities and hands-on experiments.

Book Pages
AV² pages directly correspond to pages in the book.

Key Words
Study vocabulary, and complete a matching word activity.

Quizzes
Test your knowledge.

Slide Show
View images and captions, and prepare a presentation.

AV² was built to bridge the gap between print and digital. We encourage you to tell us what you like and what you want to see in the future.

Sign up to be an AV² Ambassador at www.av2books.com/ambassador.